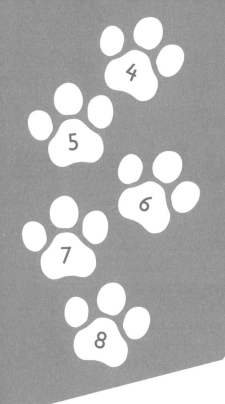

This .... to

....

....

TELLING THE TIME
Activity Book

Colour the paw print when you complete a page. See how far you've come!

How to use this PAW Patrol Activity Book

This PAW Patrol Telling the Time Activity Book has been written to provide an introduction to telling the time. This book introduces the basic concepts of telling the time, including the units of time, times of day, and how to read analogue and digital clocks.

- Find a quiet, comfortable place to work.
- This book has been written in a logical order, so start at the first page and help your child to work their way through.
- Read out the instructions to your child where necessary and make sure that they know what to do.
- End each activity before your child gets tired in order to ensure that they will be keen to return to the activities next time.
- Help and encourage your child to check their own answers as they complete each activity. (Answers can be found on page 24.)
- Let your child return to their favourite pages after they have completed them. Talk about the activities they enjoyed and what they have learnt.
- Remember to give plenty of praise and encouragement.
- Once your child has completed all the activities in the book, reward them for their effort and achievement with the certificate on page 23.

Let the PAW Patrol help you with Telling the Time!

PAW Patrol – here to help!

ACKNOWLEDGEMENTS

Published by Collins
An imprint of HarperCollins*Publishers* Ltd
The News Building, 1 London Bridge Street, London SE1 9GF
1st Floor, Watermarque Building, Ringsend Road,
Dublin 4, Ireland
© HarperCollins*Publishers* Ltd 2022
10 9 8 7 6 5 4 3 2 1
ISBN 978-0-00-852642-9

The author asserts the moral right to be identified as the author of this work. All rights reserved. No part of this publication may be reproduced, stored in a retrieval system, or transmitted, in any form or by any means, electronic, mechanical, photocopying, recording or otherwise, without the prior permission of Collins.

British Library Cataloguing in Publication Data

A Catalogue record for this publication is available from the British Library.

© Spin Master Ltd. ™PAW Patrol and all related titles, logos, characters; and SPIN MASTER logo are trademarks of Spin Master Ltd.
Used under license. Nickelodeon and all related titles and logos are trademarks of Viacom International Inc.

Consultant: Carole Asquith
Publisher: Fiona McGlade
Project editor: Katie Galloway
Cover design: Sarah Duxbury
Internal design: Ian Wrigley
Layout: Rose & Thorn Creative Services Ltd
Production: Karen Nulty
Printed in Great Britain by Martins the Printers

Contents

Time words...4

Numbers on a clock (1–12)..........................6

Seconds, minutes, hours and days..................7

Morning, afternoon and evening....................8

Daytime and night-time 9

Telling the time.................................10

O'clock..12

Half past 14

Quarter past.....................................16

Quarter to 18

Digital clocks and AM and PM.....................20

Time puzzles 22

Certificate......................................23

Answers 24

Time words

Draw lines to match the time words with the activities.

I second

How long you might have for lunch time at school.

I hour

How long it takes to put on your shoes.

I minute

How long it takes to clap your hands.

Ask a grown-up to time you doing these activities, then write how long it takes in the box.

It takes ⬜ **minutes** to eat my breakfast.

It takes ⬜ **seconds** to write my name.

How long will it take Rubble to jump over a ramp? Tick (✔) the right box.

30 seconds

30 minutes

30 hours

How long will it take Chase to sneeze? Tick (✔) the right box.

2 seconds

2 minutes

2 hours

How long will it take Skye to fly around Adventure Bay? Tick (✔) the right box.

3 seconds

3 minutes

3 hours

Numbers on a clock (1–12)

Practise counting to 12 by adding the missing numbers to the number lines.

1 2 3 ☐ 5 6 ☐ 8 9 10 ☐ 12

1 ☐ 3 4 5 ☐ 7 8 ☐ 10 11 ☐

☐ 2 3 4 ☐ 6 7 ☐ 9 ☐ 11 12

1 2 ☐ 4 ☐ 6 7 8 ☐ 10 ☐ 12

Seconds, minutes, hours and days

There are 60 seconds in a minute.

There are 60 minutes in an hour.

There are 24 hours in a day.

For each group of times below, tick (✔) the longest time and circle the shortest time.

6 seconds ☐   6 minutes ☐   6 hours ☐

3 days ☐   3 minutes ☐   3 hours ☐

10 hours ☐   10 minutes ☐   10 seconds ☐

2 hours ☐   2 days ☐   2 seconds ☐

Morning, afternoon and evening

Morning is the time before 12 o'clock midday.

Afternoon is the time after 12 o'clock midday.

Evening is the time after about 6 o'clock.

Tick (✔) the correct word to complete each sentence about when the pups do their activities.

The pups get up in the:

morning ☐   afternoon ☐   evening ☐

After lunch, the pups go to play in the park for the:

morning ☐   afternoon ☐   evening ☐

Rubble has a bath and gets ready for bed in the:

morning ☐   afternoon ☐   evening ☐

Daytime and night-time

Circle the things that Ryder and the pups do in the daytime. Tick (✔) the things that they do at night-time.

Telling the time

A clock shows 12 hours.

The clock hands move in the direction of the blue arrow that Chase is following (clockwise).

Follow the arrows around the clock. Point at each number and count 1 to 12.

Write the missing numbers on the clocks.
Remember to follow the arrows so the
numbers are in **clockwise** order.

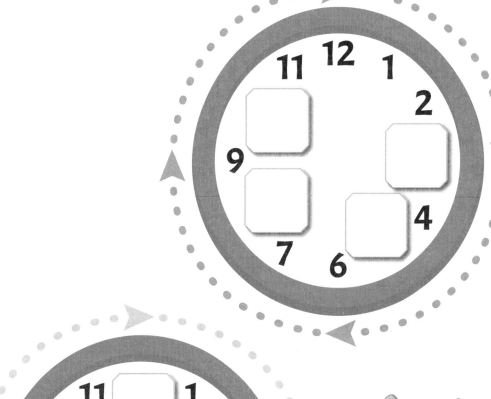

O'clock

When the minute hand points to 12, the time is **o'clock**. On this clock, the hour hand is pointing to the 4 so it is 4 o'clock.

The long hand is the minute hand. It tells us how many minutes have passed.

The short hand is the hour hand. It tells us what hour it is.

Complete the times that these clocks show.

_____ o'clock

_____ o'clock

Draw the hour hand on the clocks to show the correct time.

3 o'clock

5 o'clock

8 o'clock

10 o'clock

Half past

When the minute hand points to 6, the time is **half past** the hour. On this clock, the minute hand is pointing to 6, and the hour hand is between 2 and 3, so it is half past 2.

The hour hand is between 2 and 3. So the hour is still 2 because the hand hasn't reached the 3 yet.

Half past means the minute hand has gone halfway around the clock (the hour is half gone).

Complete the times that these clocks show.

half past ☐   half past ☐

Draw the minute hand on
the clocks to show the correct time.

half past 4

half past 7

half past 9

half past 1

Quarter past

When the minute hand points to 3, the time is **quarter past** the hour. On this clock, the hour hand is just past the number 8 so it is quarter past 8.

Quarter past means the minute hand has moved a quarter past the hour.

Complete the times that these clocks show.

Quarter past [   ]

Quarter past [   ]

Draw lines to match the time on the clock to the time given in words.

Quarter past 11

Quarter past 2

Quarter past 7

Quarter past 9

Quarter past 4

Quarter to

When the minute hand points to **9**, it is **quarter to** the hour. On this clock, the hour hand points to the number 5 so it is quarter to 5.

Quarter to means the minute hand has to move another quarter around the clock to get to the hour.

Complete the times that these clocks show.

Quarter to [   ]

Quarter to [   ]

Draw lines to match the time on the clocks to the time given in words.

Quarter to 12

Quarter to 2

Quarter to 7

Quarter to 4

Quarter to 8

Digital clocks and AM and PM

Digital clocks show the time using numbers.

AM means the time is in the morning.

PM means the time is in the afternoon or evening.

These numbers show the hours.

AM
PM

7 : 3 0

These numbers show the minutes.

On this clock, the number of hours is 7 and the number of minutes is 30. So, it is 7:30 (half past 7).

In the boxes below, draw what you do at 7:30 AM and what you do at 7:30 PM.

7:30 AM	7:30 PM

Read the time on each digital clock. Then look at the picture and tick (✔) the AM or PM box to show what time it is.

AM
PM
8 : 0 0

AM
PM
1 1 : 0 0

AM
PM
1 0 : 3 0

AM
PM
9 : 0 0

AM
PM
1 1 : 3 0

AM
PM
4 : 0 0

Time puzzles

Everest is at the top of Jake's mountain at 10 o'clock.

→

An hour later, she has got to the bottom!

→

Show the time that she gets to the bottom of the mountain on the clock.

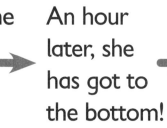

Ryder and the pups have a party at 3 o'clock.

→

An hour later, the party has finished.

→

Show the time that the party finishes on the clock.

Rubble and Marshall start to build a sandcastle at 1 o'clock.

→

An hour later, the sandcastle is finished!

→

Show the time that the sandcastle is finished on the clock.

This badge is awarded to

....

Age ....

For successfully completing

PAW Patrol
Telling the Time
Activity Book

Date ....

Signed ....

Well done!

Answers

Page 4

1 second – How long it takes to clap your hands.

1 hour – How long you might have for lunch time at school.

1 minute – How long it takes to put on your shoes.

Child's own times.

Page 5

30 seconds ✔

2 seconds ✔

3 minutes ✔

Page 6

1 2 3 ④ 5 6 ⑦ 8 9 10 ⑪ 12
1 ② 3 4 5 ⑥ 7 8 ⑨ 10 11 ⑫
① 2 3 4 ⑤ 6 7 ⑧ 9 ⑩ 11 12
1 2 ③ 4 5 ⑥ 7 8 ⑨ 10 ⑪ 12

Page 7

(6 seconds) ☐   6 hours ✔

3 days ✔   (3 minutes) ☐

10 hours ✔   (10 seconds) ☐

2 days ✔   (2 seconds) ☐

Page 8

The pups get up in the morning.

After lunch, the pups go to play in the park for the afternoon.

Rubble has a bath and gets ready for bed in the evening.

Page 9

Page 11

Page 12

7 o'clock

2 o'clock

Page 13

3 o'clock   5 o'clock

8 o'clock   10 o'clock

Page 14

half past 5

half past 9

Page 15

half past 4   half past 7

half past 9   half past 1

Page 16

quarter past 10

quarter past 3

Page 17

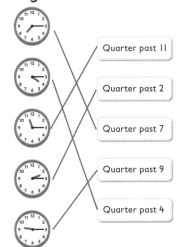

Quarter past 11

Quarter past 2

Quarter past 7

Quarter past 9

Quarter past 4

Page 18

quarter to 6

quarter to 1

Page 19

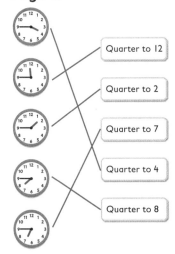

Quarter to 12

Quarter to 2

Quarter to 7

Quarter to 4

Quarter to 8

Page 20

Child's pictures of what they do.

Page 21

AM ✔ 8:00   PM ☐ 11:00

PM ✔ 10:30   AM ☐ 9:00

AM ✔ 11:30   AM ✔ 4:00

Page 22